The Cosmic Playbook for Writers:

Daily Affirmations And

Mindfulness For Authors

P.K. Davies

THE COSMIC PLAYBOOK FOR WRITERS

Reader reviews:

"This should be in every writer's toolkit! This book is short enough to read every day to inspire and motivate, or pick and choose those that apply for the day. I was pleasantly surprised at how deep these affirmations are, and even more surprised at how they made me feel. I will definitely be incorporating them into my daily writing needs."

Christine Copper, author of Goals Master Plan

"This book warmly guides you to write the book you want and to not be afraid. It helps you understand the reason for writing your own book and helps you around the thoughts that may cause us to stop. It is such a beautiful invitation to keep writing."

Lesia Zablockij, Author of Soul Fire Café

"I loved the gentleness of the meditations."

READER'S FAVOURITE (5 STARS)

JOYFUL LIFE MASTERY BOOKS

Copyright © 2020 by P.K. Davies

www.JoyfulLifeMastery.com

ISBN: 978-1-7770525-3-9

All rights reserved. No part of this publication may be reproduced, distributed, or transmitted in any form or by any means, including photocopying, recording, or other electronic or mechanical methods, without the prior written permission of Joyful Life Mastery, except by a reviewer, who may quote brief passages in a review.

For information about special discounts for bulk purchases, please contact Joyful Life Mastery at JoyfulLifeMastery@gmail.com.

Book Website and Newsletter:

www.joyfullifemastery.com

Socia Media:

https://www.facebook.com/joyfullifemastery

For writers everywhere...

Share your magic!

"We write to taste life twice, in the moment and in retrospect."

ANAÏS NIN

Table of Contents

Introduction	1
1 - Integrity	11
2 - On Feedback and Reviews	14
3 - Release It!	17
4 - Down Time	22
5 - Pacing and Routine	26
6 - I Allow!	30
7 - Mastering Distractions	34
8 - Create	38
9 - My Words	41
10 - Sharing My Work	44
11 - Going Public	47

12 - My Readers 51

13 - Authenticity 55

14 - My Best 58

15 - Appreciation 61

16 - Writer Community 63

17 - Overwhelmed No More 66

18 - A Bestseller Mindset 71

19 - Work-In-Progress 75

20 - My Work 77

21 - Marketing 80

22 - Free vs Paid 86

23 - Selling 92

24 - Sales and Downloads 94

25 - New Ideas 96

26 - Support 99

27 - Hello World! 103

28 - My Voice 105

29 - Contribute 107

30 - My Goals 110

Thank You 113

Vital Affirmations for Writers 114

Clearing & Energizing Affirmations for Money and Abundance (for Writers) 124

About P.K. Davies 130

INTRODUCTION

Welcome to *The Cosmic Playbook for Writers*!

The Cosmic Playbook offers an intentional blend of mindfulness and focused, short, positive affirmations that expand into mini meditations.

In *The Cosmic Playbook for Writers*, we dive into the realities of being a writer. Each little chapter helps create a mental and emotional reset so you can refresh whenever you desire.

One thing is certain – writing is one of the most intimate experiences you can share with readers. In fact, your writing is an invitation into your world. Your words and works are your creations - your children.

A writer's way lies in the fragile balance of outpouring, withholding and sharing. It shifts or flows through the gentle or not-so-gentle nudge of boundaries.

Writing is often a vulnerable sharing. You, as a writer, open yourself up to the world even through a pen name.

Your words tiptoe, linger, float and gallop through your world. They invite the reader on a journey from the depths of humanity's darkness and struggles to sharing and connecting through life's profound beauty and into the heart of human compassion.

And within the context of non-fiction, we discover your clear voice and your helpful guidance.

Your craft evolves through your intentions and your routine. And your words bring hope to humankind for each of our hero's journeys.

There are some unique challenges we writers face, which are part of the artist's struggle.

- You have a heartfelt desire to connect and share, whether it's through your stories or through works of guidance and support.

- You feel the panic of trying to get the words out as fast as they flow from your thoughts and inspiration, and there never seems to be enough time.

- You're caught in a battle between a deep desire for your books to be discovered and the craving to live privately and just write.

- You are a sensitive soul – critical feedback can ravage you and stop you in your tracks.

- You're not sure how to break through the times that words and ideas aren't flowing, and creativity seems to stall.

- If you're an indie writer, you're often overwhelmed by the sheer number of tasks and steps required to bring your written work out into the world.

- Not many around you seem to understand what's involved in being a writer.

- It's a real challenge juggling a day job, family life *and* writing deadlines!

In the Cosmic Playbook for Writers, we will walk through these together in the context of mindset and intensions. Here's a taste of what we will resolve through each mini meditation:

The angst of going public and being seen.

The insecurities we face about our writing quality.

The contradictory fear of both being discovered and undiscovered.

Stepping into a public image for readers who subscribe to our email list.

How to deal with poor reviews.

How to deal with writers' block and other constraints.

How to switch into a marketing and advertising mindset.

How to stay fresh and excited about our creative work.

If these mind-crowding stresses sound familiar, stay with me - we're going to walk boldly through all of these with the simple act of intentional visualization.

In fact, picture this....

Pre-Covid: You're in a public space having a little break. You're minding your own business and reading a book. Someone stands nearby, crowding your space. Somebody else sits next to you and begins speaking loudly on their cell phone.

Yet another individual comes by and stands way too close to you. You're hemmed in on all sides and you feel like the walls are closing in on you. All you want to do is get away.

You close your eyes for a moment. You breathe in deeply and let everything be. For a few minutes, you shut out the noise and disturbance. You focus on your breath.

When you open your eyes again, you feel calmer. Much calmer. You get up and stride through the crowd and find a new expansive space.

This little book will help you break free mentally from writer troubles crowding in on you, so you can refocus, recharge and get back to creating!

My name is PK Davies and like you, I'm a writer. I've struggled with all the things that crop up on the writer's journey.

When we get caught up in the panic of writing duties, deadlines and other urgencies – not to mention diving into the art and craft of writing itself - boy oh boy, can things feel dramatic!

The *good* news is that you can lovingly pick yourself up each time from a crisis or overwhelm and keep going.

The *great* news is that you can refresh yourself again and again.

You can read these mini meditations all at once, or keep them handy and read a few each day.
You can also skip to the ones that you need more at any given time.

One last word about The Cosmic Playbook meditations – these are non-religious. By that I mean, you can be from any religious or spiritual background - or you can be an atheist and still enjoy them.

The Cosmic Playbooks are created to connect us through the wondrous and remarkable shared aspects of humanity and our desire to unleash our beautiful possibilities.

One more thing...as a writer you may find your writer-mind noticing typos or grammatical errors in this book! If you do, feel free to pop me an email as I'm always delighted to improve my writing and I'll update it.

And now, allow yourself to ignore all thoughts of syntax and content and simply float on the words - allow them to carry you into a place of peace and encouragement.

At the end of this little book are two extra sections...

The first is a set of 100 Vital Affirmations for writers to help you consistently refocus on your path inward and forward!

The second is the script for a Clearing & Energizing Abundance meditation (specifically for writers).

All right my friend, are you ready? Then let's dive in!

1 - Integrity

I WRITE WITH INTEGRITY!

Isn't this a simple affirmation?

Yet within its core lies the heart of my deepest fears.

To be able to shut out society's noise and the critic of my mind, and just write what needs to emerge from my muse and my soul.

I breathe in.

I breathe out the fears, the insecurity, the unknown.

I breathe in deeply. I breathe in the energy of *allowing*.

Today, I allow myself to make mistakes. The grammar, the spelling, the misuse of phrases! Today I will let everything settle and just be. There's plenty of time to edit later.

I recognize that my decision to write may be a desire to express myself or to simply connect with the world through the medium of writing.

I put myself out there sometimes willingly, other times not so much.

None of that matters now.

What matters is that from this day forth I share my words with integrity and by staying true to my intentions.

2 - On Feedback and Reviews

I REBOUND QUICKLY AND GET BACK TO

WRITING.

Ah, feedback and criticism.

Some are meant to help, others not so much.

Some offer new perspectives and pathways to greater growth.

Others simply hurt my heart.

I breathe in calming, soothing energy.

I breathe out any pain and anger.

I breathe in universal support.

I breathe out what needs to be released.

Ooof! Out it goes.

I hold myself close and remember that it's okay.

I can accept what I choose. I can make of it what I please.

I can ignore what I want.

They are not a reflection of me as a person.

They are not an indication of the writer-in-progress that I am.

My fresh intention, right here, right now:

Each day, in every way, my writing gets better and better.

3 - Release It!

I FIND THE GIFTS AND RELEASE THE REST.

Now that I realize that feedback and criticism do not define me as a person or even as a writer, I breathe in the freshness of hope and possibilities.

I rest into this moment knowing that I can choose to turn all of this into a gift.

With a clearer mind and perspective, I sift through the feedback, the criticism, the edits. I place my focus on my book and compare each note against my work.

Those that are completely devoid of benefit – I release with relief into the Universe. Off you go! Phew!
Breathe in and out.

Now, for the rest.
Is there a golden nugget of something in this feedback that I can edit into my writing to make it even better?

Yes?

Then that's what I'll do!

Is there a hint that tells me what could be improved?

Is it valid?

Is it true?

If not, buh-bye!

But if it is...alright, I accept it, thank you!

Too short. Can I create more?

Too long. Can I distill?

The grammar is bad and there are typos. Can I edit again?

The cover is meh. Can I order a sparkling new cover?

The plot doesn't work. Can I regroup and make it tighter?

The info isn't organized. Can I clarify and rearrange?

And so it goes.

I let the feedback come my way, like bright fishes darting around me as I stand in the ocean in thigh-high water on a sunny day.

Now that I can see the possibilities, I feel giddy with delight!

I'm ready to refresh my work and make it better.

And if I can't change this book, it's okay, there's always the next one!

4 - Down Time

I USE MY DOWN TIME WISELY.

When it feels like life conspires to fill my day with drama and busyness, I take a step back.

I breathe in.

I breathe out the frantic busyness, the crowded energy and the drama.

I breathe in deeply. *Allowing, acceptance, being.*

I remind myself that this too has its message; this is a gift of time to step back and take care of business.

Perhaps there are people and things that need my attention.

Perhaps there is a message for me to replenish with self-care, to look after my health and diet and declutter everything in my life.

Perhaps this is the moment for mindfulness and quiet.

When it's truly challenging for me to write, or the ideas seems to be stalling, I accept this gift of time.

I will read and stimulate my mind with new thoughts and ideas.

I will consciously, gratefully accept 15 minutes at a time to clear the decks, replenish and refresh.

I will play.

I will look for ways to rejuvenate.

I will marvel at the skill of my colleague authors – at how they craft new ideas and worlds.

I will bide my time.

I will learn and I WILL grow stronger.

5 - Pacing and Routine

I QUICKLY DISCOVER MY OWN PACE AND ROUTINE.

Through all my challenges and commitments, I find a sliver of time each day to write!

It might via typing into an email draft on my phone on the bus or the train.

It might be by speaking into my voice-to-text app when I'm on a walk.

It might be by having that little notebook next to my bed that I can grab for a few minutes when inspiration hits.

I breathe in.

I breathe out the frustration, stress, the unsatisfied urges to write when it's not possible.... oh, I let it all go.

I breathe in deeply.

Calmness, resilience, persistence, discipline.

I'll find it where I can get it.

And I *do* find it. And I stick to it.

Even if the amount of time changes daily.

Even when the ideas swell and recede.

Even when it seems like I'm struggling to reboot my creativity.

I find it and I claim it.

That thin sliver of time builds into its own momentum.

It takes me by surprise!

And catches me in the middle of skipping through social media, or washing the dishes, or "cleaning out my emails." 😊

Time to Write reminds me that perhaps my habits are intrenched and need a little tweaking.

And that lies within my power.

I accept it now.

I will look for any opportunity to write and celebrate that moment.

For that which I give my attention to, grows stronger.

6 - I ALLOW!

I ALLOW WORDS AND IDEAS TO FLOW TO ME WITH EASE.

I breathe in, to a count of four.

In... One. Two. Three. Four.

I release my breath and any tension I've been holding inside.

Out... One. Two. Three. Four.

I'm standing in front of a golden beach. Tall palms sway above me, the swishing fronds peaceful and calming.

The sounds of the surf and seabirds are so refreshing.

Salty sea spray revitalizes my skin and I breathe in the magnificent scent of the ocean.

The sun shines down upon my body with majestic grace. I sit down with my back against a sturdy palm tree to absorb everything about this beautiful moment.

The sun's rays upon my belly loosens my muscles and the stress begins to recede. The warmth spreads slowly across my body and any lingering tension melts away. I sit and allow.

As I breathe in the salty air, I gaze upon the waves moving towards me.

I realize in this moment that the ebb, the quiet and the non-action is as necessary for my growth as the flow. The ebb and flow are in tandem, in glorious partnership. They dance into our lives and it is up to me to understand how and when to rest with the ebb, to embrace patience and celebrate it.

The flow draws fresh new creativity to me. The ebb grants me the time to enjoy and play with all that I have created, and to rejuvenate.

Sparkling lights on the waves shimmer like diamonds. Indeed, what they bring me – creativity, hope, ideas, inspiration and respite - are more precious than diamonds.

These are the gifts of Life.

7 - Mastering Distractions

I TAKE ONE FOCUSED STEP AT A TIME.

Today I will clarify my intentions as a writer and focus on my next step. Even when everything seems overwhelming,

I will remind myself to take a moment to pause and reflect, and then refocus on that next step. I'll break it down to even smaller steps if that makes it better for me.

As I do this, it gets easier. And interestingly, each set of next steps fall into place with ease on my journey.

When I need to wait for my book cover or my webpage to be created, it just so happens it's easy for me to attend to another task on my list. I take the time to play and wait.

As I focus on each step - just one at a time - it becomes easier to master distractions.

I build in a time slot just for these distractions! During that time slot, I play. I "do" social media, read my emails, tend to errands and catch up on anything else I desire.

And when that time is up, oh how refreshing it is to get back to my writing. I turn off all the distractions. I close my email Inbox and my social media accounts.

I open my notebook or document. Or I simply focus on whichever book marketing task I have chosen to work on now.

As I focus more clearly, I notice the details. In fact, the details become clearer and easier to see.

I clean up my vocabulary. I attend to the typos, knowing that my work can be reviewed again with fresh eyes.

Each focused step is in my hands.
And I deliver.

8 - Create

IT'S MY RESPONSIBILITY TO CREATE.

Breathe in. Breathe out.

I relax all my muscles.

I look down into my hands and see that I'm holding a magical box.

The box is a deep cobalt blue. Light shimmers over the blue and brings forth flickers of depth and shine. The color is breathtaking.

The edges of the box are lined with an ancient shade of dark gold. There is a push button on the front and the box has a deliciously weighty feel to it.

This box holds the key to my creative genius. I was born to create - it is in my very nature.

Each time I hold my magical box, I open it gently and release new and wondrous ideas. As the box closes, I gratefully invite Universal light and intelligence within and allow the potential to build for when I am ready again.

It doesn't matter if my work is categorized as brilliant, fun, silly or tenacious. What matters is that I continue to create.

I will share writings of value with whom I choose. That value can be academic or entertaining and I will always give it my very best effort.

I was born to create - and create I shall.

9 - My Words

I CHOOSE MY WORDS WITH CARE.

There is a reason I write each sentence. It's part of a flow, a build - it is part of the greater design of my creation.

I craft every sentence with clarity and infuse it with purpose.

Each sentence is a connection to my readers, even if that reader will only be myself.

I allow my first draft to flow like a river, crashing against the shores, moving with speed and pulling everything that needs to be released into its flow.

And then, with design and care, I revisit my work. I give my writing my attention, care, and yes, love.
I cut and carve. I move words around with the diligence of a master placing puzzle pieces where they need to be.

And yet, I rest into the assurance that all need not be perfect. I just need to work as best as I can in this moment, and search for the best team and resources that I can find.

My team are my partners - they will help smooth and pat my creation into beautiful shape so that we can release something wondrous into the world.

10 - SHARING MY WORK

I EMBRACE NEW WAYS TO SHARE MY WORK

WITH THE WORLD!

Breathe in.

Breathe out.

Every day it gets a little easier to imagine new and fun ways I can share my writing with others.

I play within my comfort zone until I'm a little too comfortable.

And then I ready myself and stretch the boundaries.

It's up to me to decide exactly how much to stretch.

It's okay - I'll figure it out. I'll grow into it.

I'll grow and I'll learn.

What I'm writing will be of value to someone.

It will inspire them, soothe them, guide them or entertain them.

It's not about me, it never was.

It's always been about *us*.

Connecting and sharing.

Opening our circles, broadening them and expanding.

Breathe in.

I will take new and exciting steps to share my work.

Breathe out.

I will adjust, I will thrive, and I will create.

11 - Going Public

The decision on going public with my writing starts with me.

Oh, the delicious agony of going public!

My stories, my words, my creations will go out into the world.

This both excites and terrifies me.

How will they be received?

Will they be loved?

Will they offer fun, hope, guidance to those who read them?

Will my book be embraced as a luscious cloak of warmth and comfort to soothe a weary reader?

Will my writing even be seen?

I breathe out my anxieties. I blow out my breath to the count of one, two, three.

I breathe in *hope*...one, two, three.

I breathe again until I feel at ease.

I allow any anxiety to freely move through me to be felt and released.

I allow any feelings of worry to move through me to be felt and released.

As my work circulates and finds my warm and loyal readers, it gets easier and easier to step out of my comfort zone and find fresh energy in change.

Change is good.

Change can be challenging - ultimately it is life-in-motion and revitalizing.

I allow myself to fall into the flow of life.

I realize that my time in this body and in this life is finite.

Yet my work – my creations - can live on in the world forever. How fun is that!

12 - My Readers

I CONNECT WITH THE RIGHT READERS THROUGH MY WRITING!

I walk slowly up a lush, green hill, my footsteps muted by the soft and plentiful grass.

I gaze around at the vast, empty spaces around me absorbing the hillside's verdant beauty.

I breathe into my heart center, slowly and with focused delight.

I breathe in sweet, fresh air. Cool oxygen fills my lungs with crystalline life-giving energy.

I look down into my cupped hands. There lie my words, pouring out from my imagination.

They rush out from my mind and my heart, a torrent blending and picking up speed as they move through me.

The words in my hands are overflowing; little bits of magic, sparkling in the light.

Words that breathe, words that thunder, words that illuminate, words that bring joy and words that draw us into reverie or adventure.

I turn slowly and sprinkle words onto the grass. Take root, beautiful little seeds and grow.
I fling them with abandon and joy into the winds.

Dance, little words!
Leap out there into the world with my blessing.
Live well, live fully.

May you attract those who are meant to find you.

13 - Authenticity

I CONNECT TO MY READERS WITH

AUTHENTICITY!

There's a magical connection between myself and my readers.

They deserve nothing but honest writing from me.

I breathe out deeply. As I do so, I release the need to appear a certain way to my readers.

I breathe in, slowly, satisfyingly. I'll just be me. The "me" that wants to serve the world and offer the best writing I can.

I fully understand the need for privacy. Yet privacy can co-exist with being authentic.

While my writing can be honest, my life itself does not have to be an open book; I will always maintain and allow the amount of privacy that I desire. And I choose where to expand those boundaries when and if I need to.

Yes, I might screw up sometimes. And so, I honor the path of my own growth as an individual and as a writer.

14 - My Best

MY READERS DESERVE THE BEST FROM ME.

There is no substitute for offering my best writing to my readers.

I don't have to aim for perfection as there is no such thing.

But I will always offer my very best.

I'll write with authenticity.

I allow my words to pour through me from my heart for my non-fiction writing.

I allow my mind and imagination to fall deep into adventure, to discover the best stories I can create for my fiction readers.

I will rewrite and edit. I will hire the best editors I can afford to help me craft my best offering.

Yes, I will make mistakes. And I'll correct them where and when I can.

I will take joy and delight in creating amazing covers for my books, or wonderful pages for my blogs and articles.

I offer my writing with respect and loving kinship to my readers.

15 - Appreciation

I'M GRATEFUL FOR EVERY NEW READER.

I send out my appreciation into the world...Dear reader, know that however you found me, I am grateful to you.

Whether it was an ad, word of mouth, or an accidental discovery – thank you for taking your time to read my words offered.

Thank you for your feedback that help my writing efforts improve or feel appreciated.

Thank you for just being there, even if you're a silent and private reader.

Thank you for supporting my writing in whichever form appeals to you.

Thank you for connecting with me, through the magical vehicle of words. Words - those little somethings that express life!

Thank you for being on this wondrous journey with me.

16 - Writer Community

I SUPPORT MY COMMUNITY OF WRITERS.

My mind boggles at the thought of just how many writers are on this beautiful blue-green jewel we call Earth.

There are SO many of us who desire to connect with readers and collaborate with other writers.

We are connected by our desire to speak and share our words.

We are so excited for readers to jump in and join us in the fictional worlds we've created and experience new and exciting adventures. We are ready to soothe and guide through our words and advice.

We are ready to inspire and delight.

We are ready to share space together as human beings through the epic energy of the written and spoken word.

There's room for all of us writers out there.

There are readers for all of us.

I reach out to other writers in the spirit of friendship and collaboration.

I enjoy the work of writers who expand my mind and views of life.

I connect with writers who create such works and I know that I will find more and more of them.

17 - Overwhelmed No More

I BALANCE WRITING WITH LIVING A LIFE.

Inhale.

Exhale.

When I feel overwhelmed, I breathe out the stress and anxieties.

I pull in my abdomen and push the air up, up, up through my body.

The stress from deadlines and the anxieties drawn from the worry of *not-doing-enough* whoosh out of my chest and out through my breath.

They float out there and I let them be.
I breathe out more of them.
As they're pushed out of me, I take a step back and observe them.

What do I *really* need to do next?
Are there 20 things or more?
Can I put most aside and focus on 10?
Out of those, what can I make notes on and leave for a while?

Can I narrow them down to 5?

How about 3?

Could I do just ONE of those things now?

Then that's what I'll do.

Just one.

And the next day, I'll do another.

And as those magical seeds are planted, I will enjoy my garden of Life.

I will create healthy and delicious meals.

I'll make the time to walk or exercise every day, even if it's just for a bit.

I will find time to laugh. Or smile. I'll find something useful and helpful to do for someone else.

And most importantly, I'll connect every day with my family. My friends. Those whom I appreciate.

I'll show up for Life every day.
And when I need a little rest or a break, I'll take that – with pleasure.
In the meantime, my little seeds are taking root. They're growing in the warm sunshine of my attention. They're thriving in the gentle rains of my excitement.

It gets easier to plan my writing schedule. With balance. With delight. With more and more energy.

I know what steps to take next.

And when something is being worked on, or I need to wait for a response from somewhere, I know that's okay too. There are other tasks for me to do. It's all part of my business.

As the momentum builds, so does my eye-opening and empowering career as a writer.

18 - A Bestseller Mindset

I ALIGN WITH A BESTSELLER MINDSET BEFORE IT HAPPENS.

I'm going to grow into my role as a bestselling author.

What kind of quality work would a bestselling author produce?

What sort of habits might I want to adopt as a bestselling author?

These habits don't have to be what everyone else does – I can tweak them as I go along.
I can iterate along the way.

I seek out the habits that empower my writing.
I find ways to reduce the habits that keep me away from thinking big.

The most important thing is that I produce quality writing in every way I can.
It won't be perfect.
It won't even be to everyone's taste.
But I will continue to master my craft of writing.

It's important for me to grow into the role of bestselling author by educating myself as well.

I will seek out the best training to help me craft my writing.

I will find helpful books that guide me with tips and advice.

I intend to sign up for courses that help with other aspects of my author business, like marketing and ads.

I will align myself with mentors so I can learn, learn and learn some more!

I'll search for articles that help me navigate through the choices for author websites, marketing and selling my work.

I'll surround myself with author peers who I respect. I'll find great support groups where we can encourage each other and cheer for each other's successes.

19 - Work-In-Progress

I AND MY WRITINGS ARE A WORK-IN-PROGRESS.

I breathe in.

I breathe out deeply.

I pull the breath from my core up and out.

I draw my breath in from Universal energy. In and down.

I ground myself to the Earth.

I breathe out any need to be perfect or "there yet."

It is all a flow.

I'm part of this beautiful and breathtaking continuum.

Every day, I write a little better. Every day, I grow a little more as a person.

Every day, I focus on the magic of Now. I embrace the quality of persistence and use it for my highest good.

20 - My Work

OFFERING MY BEST WORK AT ANY GIVEN TIME IS MORE IMPORTANT TO ME THAN MAKING A SALE.

A sale is good...it's great...it's wonderful!

It's a sign that someone is placing their trust in something I've created - how exciting that is!

Even though they haven't read it yet, they've trusted enough to take a chance on my work.

Or they've enjoyed something else I've written and have jumped in to enjoy this party with me!

I am so very grateful for every single reader who buys my writing or reads my free work. For I recognize that their time is precious - it's a beautiful gift they've given me.

And I promise to always do my best by my readers. I aim to strive higher and do better with my writing.

What I offer now — will always be the best I can do now — and tomorrow I'll do better and better.

And so, on it goes - the growth and expansion - like Life.

21 - Marketing

MARKETING CAN BE FUN!

Deep breath in.

Deep breath out.

Oh, there are so many choices out there!

So many different pieces of advice and directions I can take.

I breathe out the sensation of feeling overwhelmed.

And I breathe in Focus.

Sheer - clean, crystal clear - focus.

I will plan one form of marketing for now. I'll research it, learn it, try it and play with it along the way.

Once I've mastered how it all works, then only will I look upon another path.

But I'm also flexible - I'll break that rule whenever an opportunity arises to share my work where it will be needed, desired or read with interest by my ideal readers.

No spamming needed.

Just friendly sharing.

First, I'll start by learning general and gentle overviews of the best marketing steps to take. I don't have to follow; I can question, I will test, and I will adjust freely along the way.

Next, I'll set myself up with a simple plan. Perhaps that plan will be learned from experts, perhaps it will be a result of my own research, perhaps it will be that which falls into my path, for which I will take delighted action.

It's okay.

Everything will work out.

And I remind myself again: *Just take one step at a time, dear heart.*

Let it be study, at first.

Let there be learning.

Let there be understanding.

Let there be tests and trials and lessons.

And then, let the light of understanding clear my brow and give a lift to my steps.

Everything – the teaching, the learning, the tests – will fall into place.

It gets easier.

And then it becomes fun.

They're just different ways to share my work - to bring it out there for the readers who are looking for it.

I breathe out.

No hawking. No peddling. No pushing. No spamming. No wheedling. No tricky little ways to slip it in here or there. Well maybe I'll make a few mistakes along the way. That's okay. I will bounce back on track!

I breathe in a new confidence, a new understanding of the paths to take.

I breathe in calmness, mastery-with-mistakes-along-the-way and increasing confidence.

And yes, I breathe in fun!

22 - Free vs Paid

I'M AT EASE WITH FREE OFFERINGS.

Free.

Paid.

Hmmm...

So many triggers around these innocent words.

So many strategies.

I stand within a pool of Universal light.

I stretch out my hands.

The light flows down into my core and out again through my hands.

Light – filled with love and compassion, free of all labels. The light that connects all human hearts.

I allow this sweet and warming light to travel through me.

Down through my body, filling my core, filling my heart.

Expanding my senses, my soul.

It's okay.

It's okay if I decide to offer free work.

It's okay if I decide to offer paid work.

It's okay if I decide to offer a mix of both.

I allow the light to trickle out again through my hands – the love for my creations is released out into the Universe.

I will settle into whatever feels right, and good for me.

Even if that changes up along my way and on my path.

What's important is that my work is read by the right readers.

That's all.

The light of abundance circulates through me now, and I allow it to flow freely for as long as I like.

The energy of whatever I offer freely will return to me in other generous ways.
But that's not why I offer freely. I offer to allow the flow of creation to move through me. And I allow when and where I offer it for free.

And with just as much confidence and love for my work, I will offer my writing as paid. Whenever I choose.
It's okay.

It's my decision always.

Free. Paid.

It's all good.

They both have their place – and I will decide when and where that is.

With advice or without.

With training or without.

With coaching or without.

And even strategies can be fun! Why not try a few?

It's all good.

It's better than good...it's wonderful.

It's better than wonderful...it's fabulous and I will enjoy every minute of it!

23 - SELLING

I FIND UNIQUE WAYS TO SELL OR SHARE MY WRITING.

There is magic in the Universe.

I'm discovering fun and interesting ways to celebrate and sell my writing, and there is more yet to discover!

I open myself to interesting collaborations and new ideas.

In fact, I'll start making notes and plans.

I'll write down all my ideas and lovingly consider each of them.

The more I do that, the more ideas I will receive.

I'll attract people, articles, books and more with great suggestions and ideas.

I'll go through all of them with healthy curiosity.

And I'll start trying one of them now.

Yes, I'm going to have fun with this!

24 - Sales and Downloads

I'M GRATEFUL FOR EVERY BOOK SALE, SHARE, REVIEW CR DOWNLOAD.

With all my heart. I send thanks to my readers and customers out there in the world.

Thank you for buying my book, I appreciate you and hope you enjoy it!

Thank you for sharing it with your friends, I so appreciate your time and thoughtfulness!

I thank you for every review. The kind ones, the sweet ones, and yes, even the not-so-great-ones. I'll incorporate any constructive feedback into my work - so thank you for that! And if the review was not constructive, I banish it from my mind right now! Bye!

Thank you for downloading my article, my novel, my books, my work.

Thank you for your trust and your time.

25 - New Ideas

NEW WRITING IDEAS COME TO ME EASILY.

Goodbye Writer's Block. I release you!

Yes, you. 😊

But first, thanks for giving me a little time to rest and take care of other business.

Thank you for reminding me that I love to, NEED to, write!

Ohhhh yeah...I'm ready!

I breathe out any sense of heaviness or stagnation from my abdominal area.

I breathe in freshness, vitality and new ideas!

I let my body relax.

The ideas are coming my way, no need to stress or fret about how fast they come or not.

I welcome all the ideas.

I have my apps ready on my phone so I can store them or jot them down.

I have a notebook and pen next to my bed.

I am SO ready.

I capture those little mischievous imps - thoughts and ideas - that scamper into my mind and giggle on their way out.... gotcha!

26 - Support

I SURROUND MYSELF WITH THE RIGHT SUPPORT SYSTEM.

From this moment onwards, I release all that does not support my writing.

I will take care not to jump to conclusions but gauge the situation carefully.

If those who are not supportive include family or loved ones, I will simply become more judicious about what I wish to share with them about my writing. Maybe I'll keep it to myself until I hit Publish!

I love them and care for them, but I understand that it is what it is.

I pay attention now to the feedback I receive from all quarters.

Is the feedback for the good of my writing? Yes? Then I embrace it.

Is this person supportive of my writing?

Yes? Then I'll embrace their support.

Does this or that habit support my writing?

If no, I'll find ways to reduce those habits.

If yes, I'll find ways to increase those habits!

Little by little and step by step.

I expand my idea of *support* to include self-care.

Am I feeding myself the right foods? The right beverages?

Am I getting enough sleep? Enough rest? Enough exercise?

Am I able to make time to write?

Or am I pushing myself too much to write?

From this moment onwards, I claim my place and space in the world.

I embrace the seesaw of allowing peace and leisure on one end and the tremendous bursts of creativity on the other.
I know when to tame them.
And I know when to ride this seesaw to help me grow.

27 - Hello World!

I CELEBRATE EACH PIECE OF WRITING I LAUNCH INTO THE WORLD.

Oh, nervous excitement flutters up my belly and into my smile.

Small piece, medium piece, non-fiction, fiction, article or book — all of you are my babies and I'm about to release you into the world!

I release each of you gently, excitedly, nervously.

You were crafted from a spark in my mind and nourished with attention. You grew strong from edits and were tempered with love.

Here's to You!

May you find the readers who love you.

28 - My Voice

I SHARE MY VOICE WITH POWER AND COMPASSION.

I have discovered as a writer that my voice extends far beyond my written work.

I pause to examine and appreciate this moment; to really understand what this entails.

Breathe.

Breathe.

Breathe.

I'll be mindful of what I voice.

It's okay if I make mistakes - I'm human.

I remind myself I have a voice now as a writer and I will learn along the way.

I will do my best to share my voice where it matters, for the highest good.

When I have my platform, I will do my best to include with compassion, share with delight and support with the highest of intentions.

29 - Contribute

I ADD TO THIS WORLD THROUGH CREATING ENTERTAINMENT OR OFFERING GUIDANCE.

Whatever I write has a purpose.

It's the vehicle for my voice, and I use my voice with intention.

I'm a creator and I'm honored to offer my creations to the world.

Through my fiction work, I take great delight in entertaining my readers.

The plot! Oh, the twists and turns!

I dive headfirst into the delicious play of life and explore the shades of human nature in my stories.

I've added something of value to the world for readers who desire to be entertained.

Through my non-fiction work, I help, educate, guide, or soothe others. My desire to assist connects me with those who desire this help.

Everything I offer has a place now in the world.

And my heart is full.

30 - My Goals

AUTHENTICITY AND CONNECTION ARE MY

GOALS.

I stand within this moment; the Now, the

present.

Writing isn't just my finished work, the book,

the blog, the article.

Writing embodies the connected Now

moments of my voice becoming manifest.

Writing is the flow, the process, the pain and delight of discovery, the burning fire of growth, the soothing peace of be-coming.

It's the joy of creation.

It is the manifestation of my thought into form.

A form that will one day entertain someone.

A form that will make someone laugh, someone cry, someone think, someone FEEL.

Writing is the connection from my heart to that of my readers.

I thank them for sharing this moment with me. For sharing a moment in time, in their lives. Namaste, my readers, my friends.

I breathe in.

I breathe out.

Thank You

Thank you for reading this little love book for writers!

Read it again each day as a daily practice or write some of the affirmations in your journal.

Keep reading below to find your Writer affirmations!

May you share your vibrant voice and works, beautiful soul!

With love,
PK Davies

Vital Affirmations for Writers

1. I create works of value.
2. I AM a writer of integrity.
3. I rebound quickly and get back to writing.
4. I find the gifts in feedback and release the rest.
5. I use my writing downtime wisely.
6. As a writer, I have a passion for reading too.
7. I quickly discover my own writing pace and routine.
8. I find fun ways to stick to my writing routine.
9. I find time to create and write.
10. I find ways to stay disciplined.

11. I allow words and ideas to flow to me with ease.
12. I am patient and take my time to write well.
13. I take one focused step at a time.
14. I pay attention to detail.
15. I check and double check my vocabulary.
16. It's my responsibility to create.
17. I have an incredible imagination.
18. I think outside the box!
19. I choose my words with care.
20. I write with clarity.
21. I write with purpose.
22. I embrace new ways to share my work with the world.
23. The decision on going public with my writing starts with me.

24. I connect with the right readers through my writing.
25. I connect to my readers with authenticity.
26. I celebrate visionary writers.
27. I allow myself to write with emotion.
28. My readers deserve the best.
29. I'm grateful for every new reader.
30. I support my community of writers.
31. I balance writing with living a life!
32. I cultivate different aspects of my writing.
33. I align with a bestseller mindset before it happens.
34. I and my writings are a work in progress.
35. I surge forward with persistence.
36. Offering my best work at any given time is more important to me than making a sale.
37. Marketing is fun for me!

38. I'm at ease with free offerings.
39. I find unique ways to sell or share my writing.
40. I'm grateful for every book sale, share or download.
41. New writing ideas come to me easily.
42. I surround myself with the right support system.
43. I celebrate each piece of writing I launch into the world.
44. I share my voice with power and compassion.
45. I add to this world through creating entertainment or guidance.
46. I write with authenticity.
47. I celebrate connecting with readers through my writing.

48. I love all my written work.
49. I am a work-in-progress and I improve my writing every day.
50. I support my writing community always!
51. I find ways to support other writers individually.
52. It's easy for me to develop my platform.
53. I find time to work on my story plots.
54. Fresh ideas come to me with ease.
55. I believe in myself as a writer!
56. I have the courage to launch my work into the world.
57. I have the backbone to weather all feedback and the temperament not to take any of them too seriously.
58. I aim to improve myself in all aspects so it will reflect in my writing.

59. I take good care of myself.
60. I nurture the habits that support my writing.
61. I find splendid ways to create writing habits that work for me on the go!
62. I take pride in my book covers!
63. I find great book cover designers with ease.
64. I have a deep appreciation for the people in my life who support me.
65. I aim to create amazing books.
66. I create sensational characters.
67. My plots are marvelous!
68. I am humble with praise.
69. I write freely, allowing myself to let all the words flow before I edit.
70. I vanquish my doubts and fears!

71. I strive to write works that are striking and strong.

72. By writing a little each day, I win!

73. I am so grateful to be a writer.

74. I am really excited about what I'm writing now!

75. I am devoted to my writing.

76. I unleash my creativity!

77. I am at ease with my written voice!

78. I consistently give by creating great books and creative work.

79. I am grateful that there are loyal and enthusiastic readers out there for me.

80. I am grateful for my boundless creativity and I am at ease with the slower periods.

81. I intend to offer quality written works and market them in a way that aligns with my values.
82. I adore connecting with other authors and sharing guidance and support.
83. I am at ease with all feedback on my writing.
84. I create writing schedules and plans that work for me!
85. It gets easier for me to clear my mind to write after a day at work and time spent with my loved ones.
86. I take pride in my public author persona, and I have fun with it!
87. I choose mindfully the public appearances I want to attend.

88. My self confidence as a writer grows by leaps and bounds every day.
89. I find the right words to share with my email list and my other platforms.
90. No matter where I am in my writer's journey, I am grounded and grateful.
91. I remember all those who support my work and I thank them generously and frequently.
92. I circulate my writing knowledge and guidance freely.
93. I am never too old or experienced to learn more about the art of writing!
94. The more I write, the easier my words flow!
95. The more I write, the more fun it is!
96. The more I write, the better I get.

97. The more I write, the more I have to offer!

98. The more I learn, the more I share.

99. I am filled with the wonder of all I can create and share.

100. I write – with all my heart!

Clearing & Energizing Affirmations for Abundance (for Writers)

As I create more written work with increasing confidence, I clear and energize my spaces within and without.

I clear and energize my thoughts and emotions around earning money for my writing.
I allow myself to rebalance my energy and state of mind-body-spirit whenever I need to.

I clear any unwanted worries about selling my writing.
I cut the strings that tie these fears to my etheric state.

I forgive the critics from my past.

I release my emotional ties to reviews and feedback.

I disconnect them energetically from the ability to earn money for my writing.

So be it, so it is.

I forgive myself for any lingering regrets around what I have and have not written.

I release any lingering shame or longing for writing opportunities or collaborations that did not materialize.

I disconnect the energetic thread that ties these feelings to any ability to earn good money for my written work.

I release any fears of spending for my writing education.

I temper this release with a healthy respect for my money and I trust my decision as to when and where I should spend money for my further training.

I clear and release fears and worries around how much I earn in this moment for my written work.

From this moment onwards, I thank and bless all monies that come to me for my work.

I visualize a golden thread that links my books, blogs, articles and all writings.
I breathe life and love into this golden thread, and it glimmers and shines.
The golden thread grows outwards and connects to readers around the world.

From this moment onwards, I open myself up to new and fun ways to earn money for and from my writing.

I thank the first few cents and dollars I receive for my work.

For that is simply the beginning and it is feedback that my writing brings value to someone, somewhere.

I thank the universe for the opportunity to bring value through my writing.

I open myself up to new and fresh collaborations that bring value to readers.

I open myself to fun and creative ways to market my work.

I open myself to inspiring new ideas for books, stories and blogs that will invite money into my life.

All the while, I understand that money is not the end-result. Money is simply *one* reflection of the value I am creating and offering.

I open myself to allow in the flow of energy in the form of *all* types of abundance.

Each day, I will spend a few minutes thinking about ways to offer more and more written value.

Each day, I will spend a few minutes thinking about ways to offer my own form of financial support within the writing community, either through buying other writer's works, buying their training courses or similar.

Each day, I will remember that I can trust in myself and in Life.

Each day, I will ask myself how I can serve.

How I can create more, offer more, write more and EXPAND my life.

I intend to use my wealth in ways that will benefit myself, my loved ones and the world.

So be it.

So it is.

About P.K. Davies

P.K. Davies is an author, voice artist and singer, and has a degree in Psychology.

She creates Law of Attraction, manifesting and mindfulness products at Joyful Life Mastery.

PK Davies also creates guided relaxation, sleep, mystical, manifesting and affirmation audios with Enchanted Meditations.

To learn more or sign up for her newsletter, visit JoyfulLifeMastery.com.

ALSO BY PK DAVIES:

MANIFESTING FUN

THE PROSPERITY GAME SUPERKIT

VITAL AFFIRMATIONS

THE SECRET FOREST GUIDED MEDITATION

PURE PEACE MERMAID MEDITATION

GOLDEN EARTH DIVINE HEART ACTIVATION

BOOKS

THE COSMIC PLAYBOOK: 30 Vital Mini Meditations for Love, Hope and Courage

THE LAW OF ATTRACTION GAME BOOK: The Feel Great Handbook

BOLLYWOOD P.I. CALIFORNIA DREAMING as Priya Khajuria (Mystery / Action & Adventure / Humour)

To explore, visit:
www.JoyfulLifeMastery.com

Join Me!

Sign up for the author newsletter at:

Joyfullifemastery.com

Receive manifesting tips and launch news.

You can find me here on Facebook:

Facebook.com/joyfullifemastery

On Pinterest:

Pinterest.ca/joyfullifemastery

Amazon Author page:

amazon.com/author/pkdavies

Instagram

https://www.instagram.com/soundismusic/

If you enjoyed this book and believe that someone else will enjoy it and find it helpful, please consider sharing a simple blurb wherever you bought it.

Or consider mentioning this book to other writer friends.

Thank you, I appreciate it very much!